Neon Nightmares

By Linzi Quinnin

Neon Nightmares

LQuinnin@live.co.uk

ISBN: 978-1-4709-9302-3

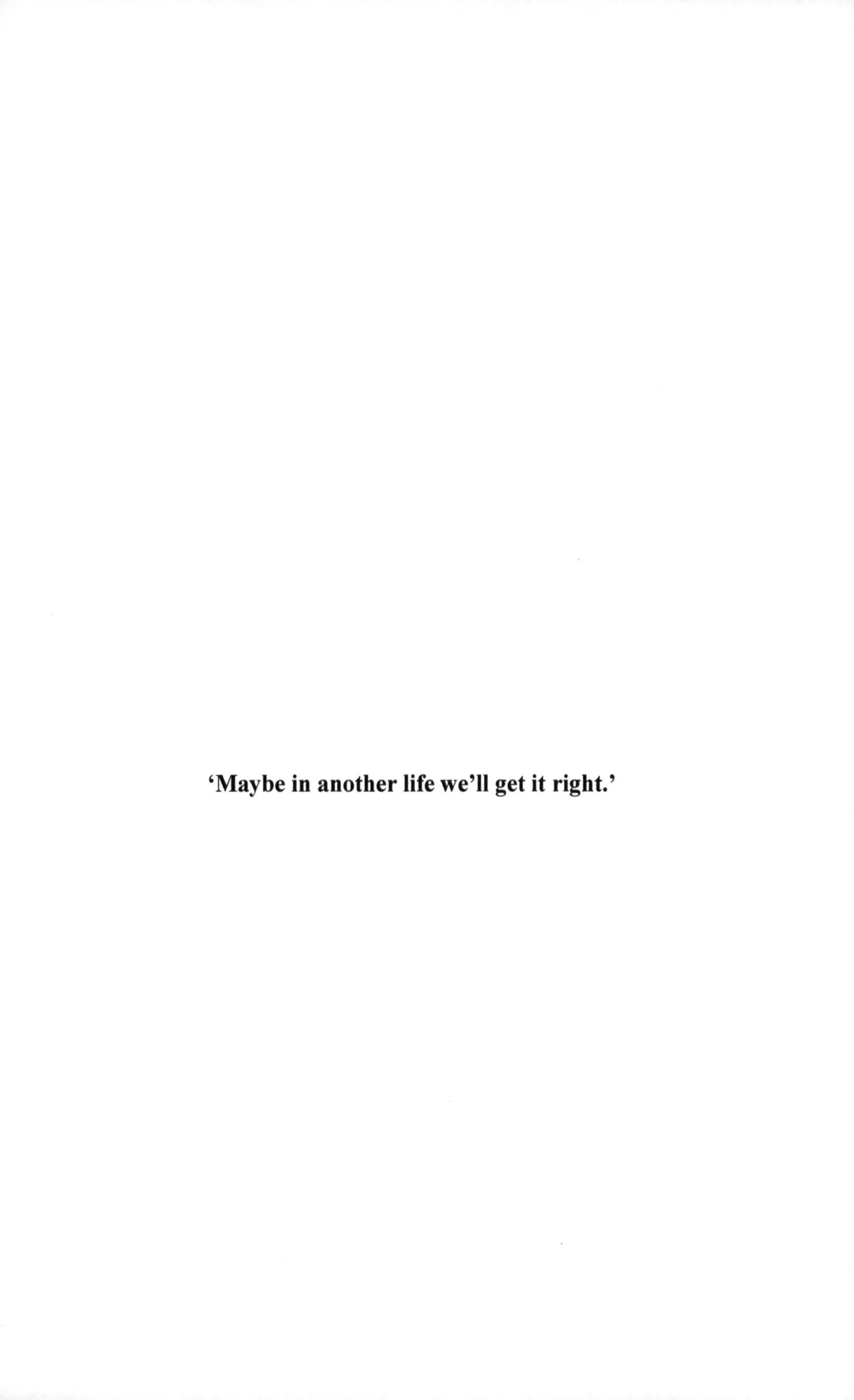

‘Maybe in another life we’ll get it right.’

Contents

Life and Death

A Dusty Dream

It stands there out of its case in a corner
Reminding me of a dream I once had
I wanted to learn and play in a band
The strings still brand new
Never really been played

They sit there on the draws
Like little wooden ornaments
A rhythm in my head never heard
Yet again the dream I used to have

I sit there in an empty room
With a broken jigsaw of memory
Bits lost and some broken
Fitting it together the best I can
It'll never be perfect
But then again, what is?
The distant notes of a failed life play
Echoing through the halls
Faded and contorted so out of shape

The rhythm of life plays randomly
Broken and out of time
The life I always dreamed
Slipping further out of my reach

So Close To Hell, So Far From Death

I came a little too close to hell that night

Sat there on your floor afraid

So cold

A new wave of despair comforted me

And I've never been the same since then

My life passed before me

The pits of my hell opened

My lies and secrets burned

Then

Something saved me

Now days are seconds, weeks are days

I have no feelings left inside me

I have no need to be here

Not now I know what awaits me

Now nothing can save me

What Have I Become?

I found myself sitting in the dark

Digging up ancient skeletons from my closet

For another night in a row

Going over my loves game

And all the pain it caused

I was thinking about the innocent heart

That I so cold heartedly wrecked

In that secret lust I craved

I was my masters' secret pet

The one behind the locked door

Not the innocent one in the game

And, in the tradition of the three fold law

The lies and secrets did fall

And crash down around me

Giving me another reason to feel

Worthless

I found myself sitting in the dark

Unable to feel anything about my wrongs

My public life documented day by day

My private life, the internet generation

The competitive nature of comparing scars

I found myself thinking

What have I become?

Memento Mori

Tabacosis caused by nicotine addiction

Cancerous lungs like sandpaper

My fragile body lacerated again

A martyr to this torture

Loss of faith in love and religion

An unheavenly self sacrifice

So many sins

I live with renegade angels

This I deserve and nothing more

In my last moments of existence

Bleeding on my death bed

With baited breath I uttered

Memento mori

Ribs

Can you see my ribs yet?

Are they poking through my skin?

No not quite

There's still a thin layer of fat

There's not long now

There not too far to go

A few more weeks should be enough

Remember that as you starve yourself

While your insides start to eat them selves

And your stomach begins to shrink

It'll all be worth it in the end

You know you'll end up stick thin

Underneath The Plastic Perfection I'm Rotten

I've done all I can to fit in

To be what they call perfect

Designer labels and a plastic chest

Despite me always hating it

And all the girls who gave in

I'm the girl who all the guys follow

The one everybody wants to know

I'm a flirt and a little bit more

Make up hides the secrets

And kisses hide the lies

Lies and Suicide

"Now cut deeper it's for the best
Drink some more, it'll help you forget
Don't eat for a few days more, I still see fat
Take some more it won't kill you yet
Don't bother calling out for help
They'll never forgive but they will forget"

The words sung by my angelic demon
The voice that plagues my mind
A depressed little girl who has it all
The body, big heart the brains and a soul
Nothing to worry about nothing at all
A walking talking stereotype
You're not sorry, no need for help

You have 9 seconds left gasping for air

Drawings on Me

My tattoos my coloured scars

Reminders of my past

Black as the ink under my skin

Reminders of all the bad

The cover up half done

The start of a sleeve on my right arm

Putting right what once was a mess

Tribal covered in stars

The hope that there's more out there

More than what's going on down here

The < 3 that lives on my left wrist

The guy who's money I burned

The days I used people for what I could get

And left once I ran them dry

The bar-coded ironic rebellion

Permanently on my right side

Against cataloguing civilisation

The date of a gig etched underneath

The day I started to play away

And fall in love behind my partners back

I hope to get my right arm finished

And have a happy memory attached

I need a little bit of sunshine

There's already too much black

I Can Show The World Your Drama

This story's on video

The whole record with audio

The whore with a heart of stone

Pleading for the drama to be famous and

I'm the best chance

At showing the world the misery

Those lies you want the world to know

You don't want to show me, show me

Show me something else

Keep talking you're so messed up

I've never seen you a deeper shade of green

Never seen you so obsessed with a deeper shade of blue

(Or the lies between me and you)

You're a masterpiece between the sheets

The evidence of your late nights is crystal clear

The evidence is picture perfect

While you're mixed up in the curtseys of tangled sheets

And I'm your only hope at being known

So why don't we dig, dig, dig a little deeper

To out how low you're willing to go

This story's growing old

The whole play with visual

The life wrecker with a heart of stone

Praying for the drama to be known and I'm

The only chance to show the world your secrecy

Those mistakes you want the world to know

You + Another Drink = Another Way to Ruin Your Life

Lips pressed close to mine

Those deep brown eyes

Your bedroom floor

Those words I'm supposed to say

I love you

The kisses I'll always remember

Cross my heart and hope to die

I'm supposed to love you

I'm meant to care

I'd say I do but simply I don't

Your alcohol slurred words

Are appealing to emotions I do not have

Appealing to times we had

But now there's too many times spent

At the bottom of a bottle

Too many nights spent on the bedroom floor

When you should have been with me instead

Now there's not a single thing you can say

To make me want to stay

You can't stand you can't think to breath

& I'm falling in love with another

While you're falling over your obsession

With another empty glass

You're just a big disaster

I'm sorry but I've felt this way all along

Crying Gets You Nowhere, It Only Gives You Something to Write About

Yet another day spent in the city centre

Wasting hours at a time by sitting around

Drinking over priced coffee in a shop

When the air con that's a little too high

Pretending to be creating the next major

Break through

With the pen and scrap book with its dog

Eared pages

When really the only thing you write about

Is another sob story poem about suicide

And lies

The one that's been told a thousand times

The same story from another failed

Wannabe writer

Love

The Player The Junkie and Two Left Feet

She's beautiful, that girl over there

I tell you now that girl's a world class player

She already thinking 'I could use another'

She an emotion junkie addicted to the rush

I can see beyond the smile and deep behind the eyes

And brother, you're her next dose

What are you saying?

I'm sure you know how the story goes

No

Ones like her play games with your body

Tease and make you beg

They know how to manipulate just right

So you give them what they want

It's player and junkie skill

They grow under your skin and firmly take hold

You'll feel like you can't let go

Mess with you until you think you love

And the nights of lust and passion will turn sour

When it all ends in regret

The whole 'relationship' boils down to

Having two left feet

And somebody is going to get hurt

And it's not going to be them

Trust me brother, you shouldn't dance

With them.

Your Love is Like Razorblades

Your love is like razorblades

Cutting at my heart

Every day in love with you

Another cut upon my arms

They burn from pain

My heart

Burns from love

Even in this torture

It's in your arms

I'll stay

Forever and a day

Headlines and Flash, Flash, Flash Photography

Overcompensate for the love I never felt

Obsess over me like you want me to be true

Paralyzed in the headlights of my stage

Watch my act, I'll convince even you

Behind the lights I look so dreadful

Make-up my pretty face hide the scars

Kiss this alter ego, hide the real me

Fall in love with what I want you to see

What I Love About You

You know what it is I love about you?

It's how I feel when I am with you

It the way your kiss makes my heart skip a beat

It's the way you hold me

Like you never want to let go

I love the way I feel safe when I am with you

It's the soft touch of your skin on mine

I love everything about you

Don't ever change a thing

And in your arms I will forever stay

It's that look you get

In those deep blue eyes

The way your kiss feels on my neck

The way I get shivers down my spine

I love the way our hellos are

And get more intense

And how the goodbyes hurt

And dig a little deeper

It's the smile upon your face

When I read your texts

It's the rain on a summer night

Caressing my pale skin

The stars, your kiss so gentile

Shining bright in my mind

My memory

The night time sky

Of how you make me feel

It's the passion in your breath

Your heart your very soul

It's the way time never slows

Forcing us apart

It's the way you make me feel

Until the time we are as one again

Inside my body and my mind

It's the way you invade my dreams

Each and every night

It's how you're always in my thoughts

I love everything about you

Don't ever change a thing

If Love Was Perfect Why Am I Alone in This Room

I sit there looking into your eyes

Knowing you think not of me

I sit there watching you move

Wishing I could feel you

Wishing I could heal you

I hear your voice

Understand the words

But I refuse to believe

The things you try to hide

In one ear, out the other

I don't want to believe

I don't want to know

You are not mine

I only wish you were

I think I can make you feel the same

Just give it a little time

I'll grow under your skin

Like a cancer unknown

Until it is too late

You can't let go

I sit and watch the way you move

And how your eyes light up

When you forget about the past

I know how you were

And how you want to be

I'm just loves casualty

Broken bones your lies

My wounds new and deep

The way I want to be with you

And it's never going to be

If This Is What I Have To Do To Find Love, I'll live With The Tile 'Slut' (Enjoy Your Wet Dream)

My face seen, so many walls

My name spoke, so many lips

My voice heard, so many ears

Love behind the lights

The stage, the fame

As real as it gets, so fake

The hearts I take, break

Fall apart in front of me

For all the world to see

Fairytale romance, cruel

The hurt of being perfect

'Webzines' show the lies

My love diminished

Crushed by rumours of you and I

Faces from the crowd

All so new and pretty

Another one night stand

My weakness looking up at me

In the thousands, something I see

Wet dreams and masturbation

Pull you out ask you in

As I stand there crying

Please hurt me

Screaming

Cause me pain

You brag on the net

I'll go find another

Tell the world you've 'had' me

Tell the world you're 'with' me

Enjoy your wet dream, I don't care

Those Little Things

When I see those little things
Strewn around the room
All those little gestures
Each make my heart sink
When I see those little things
All around your life
Every single little thing
Hurts me a tiny bit more
When I see those little things
And hear the way they talk
I know I'm not the one
Who plays on your mind
When I see those little things
And I see how much you care
I'm not the one you love
I shouldn't even care
But when you have no one else
It's kind of hard not to care
It's harder to walk away
I know I shouldn't but I do
I think I love you
Not that it matters
I'm not your one
I'm just the spare

Make-up Truths and Secret Lies

I want him to want to be with me

In the way he 'wants to be with her'

I want him to fuck me, like he does her

I don't want to sneak around

And hide for hours in his closet

I want to know that when I'm away

It is I who he wants

I'll make it so he can't get rid of me

I'll do everything he wants

I'll walk for miles see him

I want him to be mine

In the way I am his

I don't care that he loves her

And that he doesn't love me

Yet

I'll make him break her heart

But he doesn't need to know

[I'm Gonna Live in a Window] and [Share My Love With You]

I am gonna live in a window

Forever and ever and ever

I'll watch your life

As close as you watch mine

I am the internet youth

Telling tales of heartbreak

I'll show you all my lies

If you show me all of yours

Log my fears, hopes and dreams

Another same old story

I'll share every detail with you

Because you share every detail with me

And we'll play the record again

For popularity and praise

I'll fall in love with you

When you fall in love with me

Maybe One Day If you're Lucky Baby, I Might Love You

'You know how much you love me?'

He said

"No, don't say that, love is so over rated'

I said

I look deep into those eyes

They look right back at me

I

Forget to breath

'You say that like it's never going to happen'

He said

Quick reply

'You say it like it's going to happen'

I said

(Long pause)

I've spat out those poisoned words again

Again

Silence

Heart pounding, still not breathing

My head is screaming

I love you

But I don't want you to know it

I don't want to (how shall I say it)

Tell you because

(Remember, breath)

I'm scared that you won't fall for me

Like I have for you

'Oh yeah? Is that the way it is now?'

He said

(I guess)

'Maybe one day if you're lucky'

He said

What Was Going For Us Anyway

Crushed by the romance of you and I

Devastated from the lies we've told

And the words to we neglect to speak

This breakup and make up attitude

Growing old

Cursed by the love of you and I

Devastated by the cold nights

And the silence in the air

The kiss me, kiss me lipstick trace

Never there

[Untitled]

[Her] Who are you my love?

The sky?

The ground?

Where are you my love?

I miss you

My love,

Shelter me from the rain

Shade me from the sun

Hold me my love

[Him] My love,

Life would not be the same

If it were not for you

Your beauty still takes my breath

Away

My love,

You stole my heart

I am with you every single day

Do not cry

Dry your eyes my love

[Her] Where are you my love?

My only love I am forever faithful

I await your return

I miss you

More than the heavens are missing a star

Pray you hurry and return

So I can be by your side

My love, I crave your return

I crave for our passion

Our moonlight romance my love

And Now The Waiting is Over [I Love You]

I sleep in the warmth of your arms

Under the cover of night

Our love a secret passion

Shared in razor blade kisses

And the dreams of you and I

May my wishes be granted

Allow me to have and to hold you

I never want to have to say goodbye

Let us not take those words for granted

And together we will undo the mask

The other life that we have created

Become a public show

Our love will be a lie no more

Like a colourful parade for all to know

Amongst friends our story will be told

And the secrets will grow old

The time spent apart will bring us closer

Because I love you

Because you love me

'I'm Sorry' Sounds Empty

If only I could mend your broken heart

And fix my broken ways

You'd see how much I love you

And I wouldn't need to stray

If we continue down this path

I'll get lost in a forest of lies

I've already picked the guy

That might eventually tear us apart

I wish you didn't have these hang ups

I wish they'd go away

And it's all because I told you

About my stupid bloody past

Honesty is supposed to be the best policy

But if I'd have kept it secret

I might not have broke a vital part

I know I need to make things right

But I don't know where to start

Tell me what I need to do

Then I can make it happen

I don't think I know enough words

To talk away your mistrust

I can speak to you

But I'll never say a thing

Somehow the words

I'm sorry

Sound empty

Phone Call From The Past

I got a call from the number on the back

Of a photograph

The caller asking

How've I been?

That voice echoing through my cranium

The warning bells begin to ring

I recall all the fun I had with you

And all the nights we spent together

I shouldn't even remember your name

Yet happily I'd risk it all

For that thing that we called love

For what was nothing more than a parlour game

We've done it before

We could do it again

Step 1 Step 2 Step 3

Eyeliner lies and mascara tears

Lipstick trace on your forgotten face

I found you captivated by my side

Drowning in a sea of lies

The way you smell is left to linger

Another date with a pen and paper

Another case of one for all

And all for nothing

It's not just your fault

The lack of love is tearing me in two

Dark streets at midnight

Nothing seems quite right

Walking this empty town

Alone in my fragile mind

This lonely bedroom, curtains drawn

Follow by my side through loves lie

And the memories of me and you

We lost half the summer in the blink of an eye

I'm the one you cut your wrists to at night

In your sleep you dream of me

And the body heat we used to share

Crash Down 3 Fold

I think maybe it's time for you to see

The make-up truth behind the mask

Before I give in, drop out

The lies I've created about to undo

Crash down 3 fold on me

I'm telling you in blind desperation

I hope you'll forgive and forget

Let me make it up to you

Let me be with you like I'm supposed to...

Love you

Can my love belong to you

Can you forget the past of recent days

Go back to how it used to be

The best days of our lives

Let me take it back

Let me take you back

I'm telling you in complete desperation

I need you to forgive and forget

Let me make it up to you

Let me be with you like I'm supposed to...

Love you

Can my love belong to you

Let me take it back

Let me take you back

Before it crashes down 3 fold on me

Answers On The Back Of Postcards

You are my weakness, my craving

Those pictures, your body

Sculpted and toned

The temptation of great pleasure

You're highly contagious

Hazardous

Covered in warning

Yet still I want to feel your skin

And the deceit of

We're just good friends

These feelings are my addiction

You're the high before the overdose

The kiss before the secrets out

We're both re-creating memories

The corrupted chapters from our past

The photographs capture fake smiles

Our made up days of perfection

The nights in bed with another

We play chicken

And run across the motorway

Dodging cars until we get caught

You like a poison running through my veins

Your affection is death-wish treason

Yet I crave these feelings more

I'm addicted to this covert operation

The romance between you and me

And the body of you, the other

Sharing saliva is a fatal car crash

Bringing us closer to falling in love

Your touch creates more chaos

As you explore all over my body

The urge to be with you becomes more intense

I'm in love with the danger

The secrets

The lies

My hands hold him

My hands hold you

Our fingers are dirty with sin

My lips kiss him

My lips kiss you

And the words are coated in secret

In The Growing Secret of You and I Nothing is Sacred

The sea of romance is nothing

When compared to the mountains of pain

I now suffer because of you

Every second in your arms

Another razorblade swallowed

This lust filled want nothing but hurt

Every day a bullet in my head

Another dagger in my heart

While the secrets grow

The night grows dark

Every sunset our lie matures

And those 3 words try to escape

Dropped into the conversation

Masked with a question

I love you

Dear You

Sorry for all those stupid things we said
On your part as well as mine
Even though I know I caused this
And this pantomime charade of emotions
That chorus of argumentative words
Slipped out of my mouth
And onto the floor in a moment of bad taste
And now that spark of light has gone out
Left me feeling so empty
Dead and hollow inside
I messed with the golden sunset in your head
I turned it into a tidal wave of a devastated picture
I broke our foundation, killed the passion
You gave me your heart
And in an alcohol induced vomit
I threw up so many harsh words
And in those few moments
A feeling of pure hate formed
In the corners of my mouth
And the love I had for you
Subsided into the icy waters
In less than a second I drowned the fireworks
That were exploding inside my heart
Like rats on a sinking ship destined to drown
My sharp and spiteful tongue split us apart
Cut us into the little scraps I'm now clutching on to
In the hope something can be salvaged
I'd fix this if I thought could
But I fear my tears will never dry
What more can I do other than hope and wish
On something that I've buried under 6 foot of burning ash

When apologies sound like last second death row innocence pleas

I never meant to hurt you

I promise

I guess the only thing to comfort me

Is that I poured my heart and soul into a bottle

For you to do with what you will

Other

The Illusion of Disillusion, How We Suffer

In the absence of peace and love

In this, our world full of haste

As the disillusioned population

We crave sublunary pleasure

In a mechanical form we adhere

Parallel to one another

Yet separate

Giving into lust filled cravings

Seduction of plastic perfection

Subliminal messages fill our heads

Superficial charm, reckless decisions

Internal antagonisms prevail

Razorblade romances are useless

Forbidden passion is a slow and painful death

Political Society and Other Bits

The election is a choice of values
The choice of parties, the candidates
And of lying despising leaders
Opt out if you want
The liberal market-democratic nation
Blair-ism, if there is such a thing
The expression of ideology behind
Policies
Iraq was not an accident
With Mr. Blair all we get
Is more pen-pushing bureaucracy
But what does it matter?
After all I'm only seventeen
Not old enough to vote
So my views are pushed aside
Even if I did vote
I'd only want it back

What Do You Expect From Me? [I'm Only Living in Hell]

And what if you think I'm sour?

At least hear me out, OK?

With their views of perfection

Becoming more and more...

Idealistic

(For lack of a better word)

And with subliminal messages

Everywhere

On the TV, in papers, magazines

In my mind's eye

In my dark and awful secret

I HATE IT ALL

The pressure of society

Its' unrealistic desire to make us all alike

There is no escape from it

It's all a huge mind fuck

I kind of wonder

What does it matter if I look like everyone

Else

Right?

Why is it that we have this need to adhere?

Why are we like sheep in a flock?

Is it the latest trend to be brainwashed

Or have I just missed the punch line in a really bad joke?

'Seen kids' who think it's cool to advertise self-harm

And there so called depression

The fear that you can't go out looking flawed

Like we need to be dolled up

And dressed to the nines

The need to dress to impress

Because being ourselves is no longer enough

Fashion says stars and stripes

I have those, I'm a hypocrite,

Right?

And the newest obsession

The size 0

Needing to cover our flaws to make us desirable

Right?

If I had my choice

Things would be done differently

Life would be much better

At the minute all we have is Tony Blair

Who let's face it is an idiot

With his friendship with the amazing

George Bush

Who has his guns

And the warfare with

The pointless deaths

The nuclear weapons

'GOD BLESS AMERICA'

The vast oil consumption, global warming

Over population, MRSA, bird flu

The everyday stuff that just keeps building up

The fact that our life is a lie

The story told to make us want to fit in

The nanny culture telling us what not to eat

Because it'll make us fat

What not to take and what to do

What to believe in and where to go

Telling us how to live our god damn lives

Taking our individuality and uniting us as one

A mass produced youth from uniform fit mould

We are society's pawn in this game of life

On a larger scale; their single currency

The Euro

Everywhere we turn there is another warning sign

And here is us, the Internet generation

As we sit here pouring out our heart and soul

Sharing stories of loves hurt and the pain inside

Finding we each have something different to say

We don't matter we don't want to fit in

We are the unheard part of this democratic nation

With memories of the past and questions

About scar covered arms

With our webzine fixation the on line

Diary, our public life

Nothing is left secret, nothing is safe

With credit card fraud identification theft

And so on and so on

The common misconception about certain cults

The rumours of depression and suicide

Behind the fashion, the 'celebration' of self harm

Beware of the cult of 'emo'

How Not to Survive If You Want to Stay Different

Subliminal messages from our society

Telling us how to fit in

Showing us how to look

Wear this

Don't wear that

It's not this season

Eat this eat that

You're not attractive if you're fat

Make us all uniformed

Make us all the same

Stereotypical minds

Afraid to be different, afraid to stand out

They don't want us to be individual

(If you count hundreds of you doing the same)

They want us like them

Dull and boring, another job in a suit

Another fashion trend

Now afraid to be ourselves

Without our daily make-up

Fears of flaws

And unrealistic dreams

Of mass unification

Desires of idealistic perfection

Warp our minds until we are all the same

In The Event Of Fire

Faces

Names

People

Unknown

Horror and panic grow

Light headed

Paranoid

Frozen to the spot

Can't move

Voices talk

I hear no words

Legs seize

Mind freeze

Short of breath

Vision blurred

Labour Britain - Oh How You've Fucked Up

If part of setting a "clear direction"

Means imposing more taxes

They can forget it,

They've lost my vote

What difference does it make

If they keep Gordon on or not?

The risky option of electing a new leader

Is probably not that risky at all

Labour Britain will continue to fall

Find Me Something I like, Then I'll Believe

'All persons in this book are fictional
Any similarities between these persons
And related events in this book are purely
Coincidental'

Genesis to revelations
This story is a hoax
None of the events happened
None of it is real
God, Jesus, Joseph
The Virgin Mary
A massive conspiracy
Headed by the churches
Pointless wars
Idolization
The idea of creation
Who cares about natural selection?
Who believes in evolution?
No big bang,
No mixing of elements
Just pure old hard work
And a day of rest
10 commandments, sacred cows
Strange rituals,
Gifts of spice, flowers or goat
Holy wedding vows
Etc
Etc
The same old same old
I can't find anything I'd like to believe in
So I don't

The Four Horsemen

Moonlit trees, the woods in autumn

The cries of wounded soldiers echo

Dead leaves stir in the night time breeze

A row of candle lit death beds and open windows

The smell of death permeates the air

The prayers of many religions muttered

By the injured and the dying

A never ending plea from so many

To end their pain and suffering

The last screams of the dying haunt the room

A figure stands hidden in the deepest shadows

Patiently watching the shimmering white lights

Silently waiting for the lost souls to

Find their way

Is this 'death himself' personified?

Famine spreads and pestilence follows

As winter comes and goes the war draws

The four horsemen are still going strong

www.ingramcontent.com/pod-product-compliance
Ingram Content Group UK Ltd.
Pitfield, Milton Keynes, MK11 3LW, UK
UKHW041836200726
13854UKWH00003BA/1170